Anxious Angus

C Croft

Freedom Publishing

Copyright

Foreword

Foreword by Freedom Publishing, LLC©2025

Anxious Angus is the first in a planned series from the author, designed to engage readers of all ages in meaningful conversations about the emotional challenges we encounter both in childhood and throughout life.

What sets this book apart is its artistic approach—it features original watercolor illustrations that bring a timeless, handcrafted quality to each page. In an era of digital production, *Anxious Angus* offers a return to the classic tradition of bookmaking, where storytelling and art come together in a truly unique and heartfelt way.

Look out for upcoming books in this author's series, including: *Anxious Angus: Angus Misses Mose.*

Visit us at **www.freedompublishingllc.com** and **www.anxiousangus.com**.

Dedications

To my Mom, Dad, and Sister,

I truly appreciate your endless love, support, and generosity more than words can say. Thank you for always showing up for me and encouraging me to be my authentic self. I love you all dearly.

To my Husband,

I could not have done this without you. Thank you for your unwavering support and encouraging me to push beyond my fears. Thank you for being my home—the place I feel safest, most loved, and most myself.

To Gina,

Thank you for being such a dear friend and for the incredible gift that made this possible. You've been a shoulder to lean on and you continue to be such a blessing in my life.

To John,

I am deeply thankful that our paths have crossed. Thank you for being part of this journey with us and lending your extraordinary talent and compassion.

To Kittie,

Thank you for being so incredibly helpful, for being another set of eyes, and for offering encouragement throughout this journey. We are deeply grateful for the continued kindness and support you have shown.

To my buddy, my little peanut, Angus,

You taught me the true meaning of unconditional love—how to be more patient and how to adjust my expectations when I found myself in unfamiliar territory. I didn't fully understand the depth of your struggles with anxiety, but you showed me how to sit quietly with you and love you through it.

You have also allowed me to lean on you, offering comfort and love in unimaginable ways simply by being yourself. This journey has been possible because of who you are, and for that, I will be eternally grateful and love you forever.

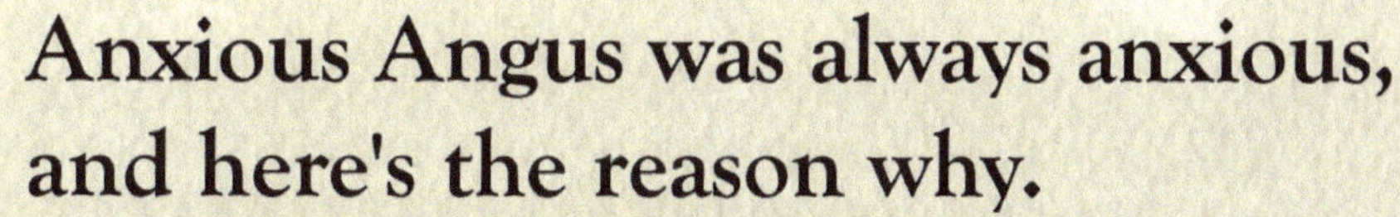

Anxious Angus was always anxious,
and here's the reason why.

His mother was unloved and mistreated
and thrown out, without a goodbye.

Angus' mom lived on the streets
and didn't feel anyone cared.

She had to find food and shelter,
which left her alone and scared.

While on the streets, she met Angus' dad,
soon to make a family and then,
with 10 pups on the way she felt unsafe,
and decided to make a friend.

Angus' mom met a
friend named Gina,
who gave lots of food
and care,
and what this taught
the momma,
was that someone
good was there.

Halliday

Although Gina shared food and showed
lots of love, the momma was slow to trust.
Then one day when the pups were born,
rescuing them was a must.

Gina and friends tried to
help the momma and all
10 pups find a home.
But the momma was
often so afraid, she
could not be left alone.

The momma built a trusting bond, so Gina
took her home, and had to help raise 10 little
pups, so they would not be left to roam.

The momma had 9 black and white pups, with only one that was tan.

That was little Angus, a sweet, but anxious little man.

The momma was
given a lovely name
and Bristol is who
she became.

She grew to be
healthy, strong and
beautiful, but
anxious still the same.

Bristol trusted
few because her
treament had
been so rough,
and some of this
she passed onto
the pups, the
belief the world
was tough.
UHalliday

Most of Angus' siblings were playful, energetic, and sweet, but some were anxious like Angus, a little fearful of who they would meet.

Soon it came time for
Bristol to say "goodbye"
to all her babes.

They all went in
different directions,
with new loving
parents and names.

Gina's good friends adopted Angus, giving him all the love he deserved, but there were moments that he continued to fear some of the world he observed.

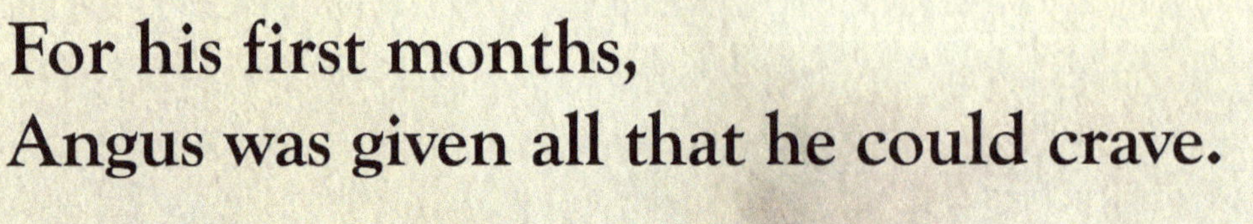

For his first months,
Angus was given all that he could crave.

He had new loving siblings to play with,
but still found it hard to be brave.

He had toys, a
nice yard, and
bones of plenty, but
was unsure of new sounds
and sights.

For the world he felt
unready, but would try
with all his might.

Angus' new family did their best
to teach the world was good,
and that it's okay to trust safe things
and hoping that he would.

As Angus was able to meet more people and
see all the good that was there, he started to
believe that he could love people because most
people really care.

Even though some anxiety and fear
was passed from momma to pup,
Angus learned that he could get through it,
and be brave just enough.

Angus' new
parents would take
him to class, so he
could make some
friends, and learn
good manners, and
self-confidence, so
some of his anxiety
could mend.

So now Angus
is big and
strong, with a
soft coat of
rusty red.

He's able to
show the
goodness in
him by holding
high his head.

As Angus grows older and learns new lessons and
experiences more and more hugs, Angus becomes
braver and braver because that is what love does.

So, although Angus can be anxious, he learned he can
be so much more, like courageous, a good brother,
and kind to others, and a dog people will adore.

Anxious Angus

From the Author

Thank you to everyone who has read and shared my book in hopes of spreading kindness and understanding in our challenging world.

I chose the pen name **C. Croft** to honor several deeply important people in my life, individuals who have profoundly shaped who I am and the work I do today. I am a licensed mental health professional, supporting individuals who are navigating anxiety, grief, chronic pain, and other personal challenges.

The story of *Anxious Angus* is inspired by my own rescue pup, with illustrations created from real photos of Angus and his family. I wanted to show that while the struggles we endure may remain part of us and our story, they do not have to define who we are or limit what our future holds. We can choose to love and be loved…and be so much more.

Illustrations

Artist, John Halliday

John's love of art and being creative started at a very young age, but it was not until later in life that John found his calling as an artist. He was introduced to watercolor painting while traveling to numerous locations abroad during graduate school. These experiences resulted in the development of a loose and understated style heavily influenced by Chinese landscape painting. He is drawn to watercolors due to their dynamic and unpredictable behavior. John has worn many hats in his work career, that includes being a nurse, designer, teacher, and ultimately a full-time artist currently residing in Mobile, Alabama.